Established 2011

1776 Fairway Drive
Courseville, USA

Site of the
Scooter Pines Invitational
Scooter Pines Women's Open
Scooter Pines Men's Open
Scooter Pines ProAm
Scooter Pines International Amateur Championship
Red Stripe Hardware National Team Championship
Colonel Bogey's Junior-Senior Championship

To the memory of George Pulver. You taught me the fundamentals of the game but also the fundamentals of life. - *D.P.*

*To my mom for never giving up.
For Ann and Walker for inspiring my passion.
And Deborah for making me realize it. - S.F.*

To Krista, my wife and best friend, for always being there for me - K.T.

SCOOTER PINES PUBLISHING
An imprint of Scooter Pines Holdings, LLC
P.O. Box 5365, Virginia Beach, Virginia 23471
Text copyright © 2012 by Dottie Pepper and Scott Fuller
Illustrations copyright © 2012 by Kenneth Templeton
All rights reserved, including the right of reproduction in whole or in part in any form.
Scooter Pines Publishing is a subsidiary of Scooter Pines Holdings, LLC.
Book design by Scott McLaughlin Fuller
The text for this book is set in Kristen ITC.
The illustrations for this book are rendered in acrylics and oils.

Library of Congress Cataloging-in-Publication Data Available
Pepper, Dottie
Bogey Tees Off/ Dottie Pepper and Scott Fuller; illustrated by Kenneth Templeton

Summary: Bogey Ballton is an ambitious range ball who is tired of his dead end job at the practice range, until John the Ball Washer helps Bogey to be Truthful with himself and pursue his life's passion to become a pro tour golf ball.

ISBN 13: 978-0-9850141-0-0

Printed in The United States of America

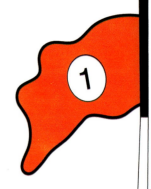

BOGEY

TEES OFF

Vol. 1 -　　　　　A Lesson About Being Truthful

Based on Characters Created
By Scott Fuller

Written By
Dottie Pepper and Scott Fuller

Illustrated by Kenneth Templeton

Scooter Pines Publishing
USA

Bogey Ballton, III wasn't your typical range ball. He had **ambition**... a fancy word that meant he wanted to do something special with his life.

"I'm willin' to do whatever it takes to get ahead in life," Bogey thought out loud, "but *THIS*... is ridiculous!"

His nose was smashed against the rear of the ball in front of him. "You didn't happen to eat beans for breakfast did ya?" asked Bogey. "You know, the magical fruit that makes you..."

"HUSH YOUR TRAP, BALLTON," barked Bucket Boss Bob. He loved yelling into his mini-Megaphone, eating red gummy sharks, and telling every ball what to do. "I DON'T HEAR ANYONE ELSE COMPLAINING!'

Bob was right. Life at the practice range was easy-peasy. Nothing dangerous about it.

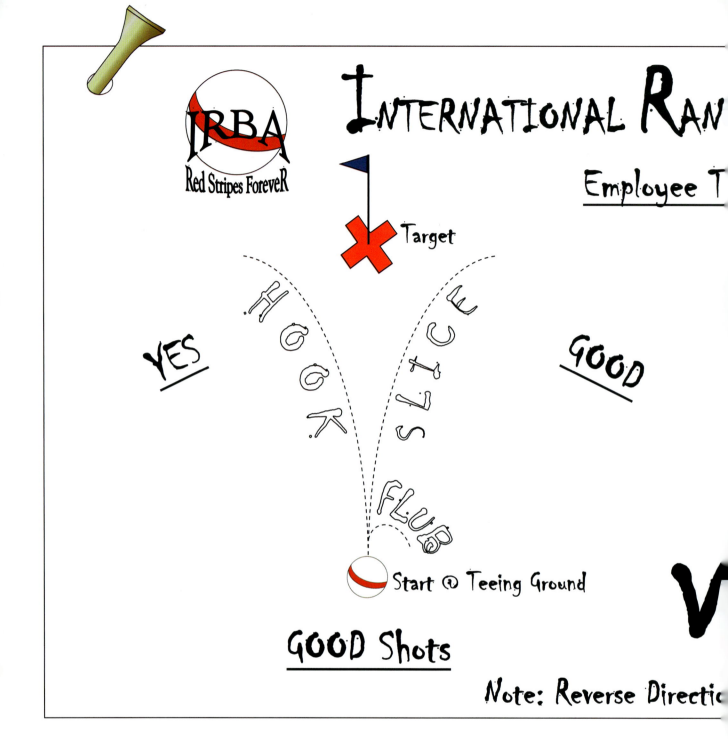

As a matter of fact, working at the practice range meant... guaranteed allowance!

Whether you hooked, sliced or flubbed when a golf club hit ya, you got paid. Even on rainy days when you didn't have to do any-

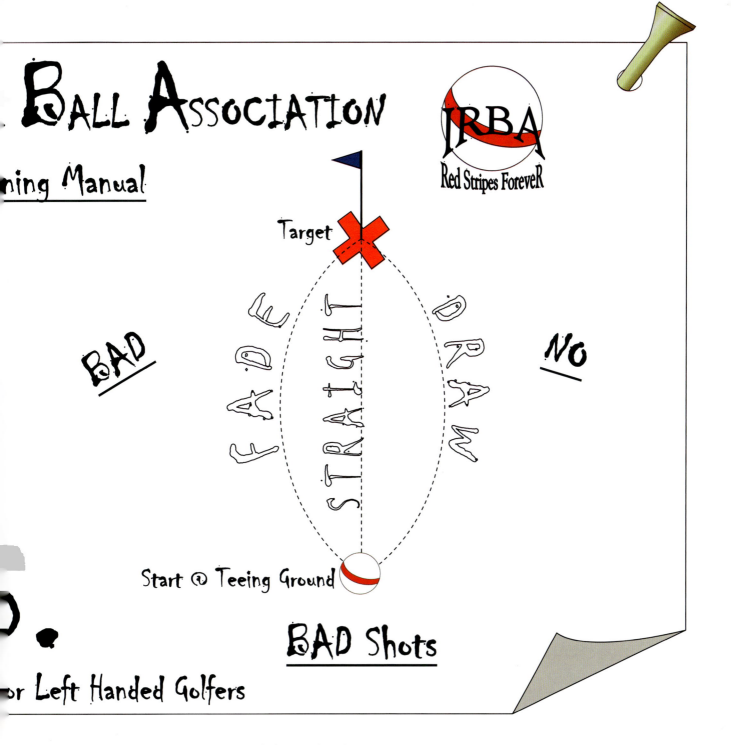

thing, you got paid. CHA-CHING!

Bad was good. Good was bad. The practice range bosses wanted bad shots to keep the golfers coming back to practice.

"Good for business," they said.

All the range balls at Scooter Pines Golf and Country Club loved their job, except for Bogey. He was tired of practicing. He wanted to play the real golf course, not the practice one. He wanted to play on the PGA TOUR!

But HOW? Range balls weren't allowed outside the practice range?... And why would they be?...

"Because I'm as good as any ball out there," exclaimed Bogey to the nervous golf tee below him.

But before the tee could remind him he had a RED STRIPE, Bogey blasted off like a rocket. He raced skyward, straight as usual and screaming at the top of his lungs - "THREE" - just to let everybody know he was comin'.

Even old Albie the Albatross knew to watch out for Bogey. "Never seen a range ball like him before," old Albie would say. "Usually, you yell FORE to let folks know you're comin' through."

—THREEEE...

Albie just figured Bogey was a typical range ball who thought FORE was FOUR and he couldn't count past three... But Bogey could count past three. He just liked to yell T H R E E because it was his number. And besides, anything worth a count always started with three! Like good music and a good golf shot... and ah-one, and ah-two, and ah-....

When Bogey eventually glided back down to earth, he landed in a bunker at the back of the practice range. He looked like a fried egg. His two best friends were waiting for him as usual.

"Where you **BEEEN** all day, amigo?" asked Tres. He was (Pronounced "Trace") a broken three wood from Mexico.

"You's late!" chipped Libber, a broken golf tee from Philly.

"Stuck in a bucket," declared Bogey. "But that's all about to **CHA-CHANGE!** I've got a plan!"

Bogey's enthusiasm spread like a wild stomach bug in a kindergarten classroom.

Tres and Libber hid behind the secret cover of a bush as Bogey returned with a jar of w h i t e make-up.

"¿Qué es eso?" asked Tres.

Bogey wasn't sure but he knew his mom used it to cover up the spots on her dimples. Whatever it was, they quickly started sponging it all over Bogey's red stripe. It started to work.

"*Top Flight School* starts in five days," Bogey announced.

"Wait ah… That's for golf balls who wanna try out for the tour!" said Libber.

"Right-amundo! And that's exactly why we've gotta hide my RED stripe and get down to Top Flight School to sign me up!" exclaimed Bogey as they dabbed on the final touches to his DISGUISE…

Just as they began admiring their handy work, a CLACKING sound rumbled in the distance. It grew louder and LOUDER!

Clack- Clack- Clack- Clack- Clack- Clack!

But before they could shout "SPRINKLER!" a giant blast of water shot through the sky and soaked all three of them...

They looked down at the white puddle of water surrounding Bogey's feet. The last few drops of make-up dripped off his dimpled body.

"Spray paint might do the trick," Bogey replied. "Maybe we can find some at my house!"

Just when all was still at the Ballton house, Bogey bounced through the front door and yelled, "MA - PA!"

He was out of breath, and of course, his parents were sitting and standing right in front of him.

"I need a can of white spray paint!" said Bogey.

Ma Ballton asked if he'd checked out back in the bunker. He had. Bogey seemed to be out of luck. He turned to his Pa.

"Don't look at me, son," said Pa Ballton. "We're range balls. We live in a shoe box not a hardware store."

"And before you roll off and try to find some, my little dimple-britches," said Ma Ballton, "that pet divot of yours has been up on my clean couch again. He left another GIANT GREEN GRASS STAIN. You need to take him for a looong walk!"

"UhhggG!!!" moaned Bogey.

"Excuse me?" said Ma Ballton.

"Yes, ma'am," said Bogey as he wobbled toward the front door.

Skid Markz jumped up with a muddy bark and followed Bogey out with a wag of his grass...

As the sun set over the Scooter Pines practice range, Bogey, Tres, and Libber slid Skid Markz back and forth around the neighborhood. Bogey explained how they would roll down to the hardware store after work the next day and buy a can of white spray paint. "Even if it takes all of my allowance!" Bogey declared.

It sounded like a great plan as they wobbled past more shoe box houses.

Skid Markz barked in agreement but not before leaving a little dirt ball on the cart path.

Of course, Bogey had to pick it up. All he could say was, "UhhggG!!!

The next day, Bogey rolled as FAST as he could down to the hardware store. He practically knocked over Big Red's bubblegum machine when he got there.

"Good afternoon, Gentlemen," said Big Red. "What's all the hulla-balloo about?"

"Spray paint! We need a can of white," said Bogey. "My future depends on it!"

"Ah, shucks, fellas. I'm afraid y'er outta luck," said Big Red. "I wish I could help ya. The RPA won't let me sell spray paint or any kinda paint for that matter anymore."

"The R-P-A?" asked Bogey.
"You know, the Range Protection Agency," whispered Big Red. "They're hurtin' my business."

"Mine too!" said Bogey. "What's this Country Club coming to?!"

And what was Bogey supposed to do NOW?!...

Once outside the hardware store, Bogey's disappointment changed when he spotted the purple neon **SIGN** across the street.

It read: **DOCTOR BALLPIN'S 30 MINUTE MIRACLE COSMETIC SURGERY**

Wasting no time, the trio ran inside. The only other ball in there was a tennis ball with crisscrossed string marks tattooed all over his body. He looked like he'd been attacked by a waffle iron.

As the nurse escorted him to the back, Bogey overheard her say,

"In thirty minutes, you're gonna look and feel like a brand **NEW** ball!"

Bogey quickly turned and addressed the receptionist with an eager smile...

She said, "next!"

"I'm afraid that's impossible," said Dr. Ballpin. "Even if my thirty minute miracle machine could perform such an operation, I wouldn't be allowed to do it. It wouldn't be Truthful. And, if I could do it, you'd still be a range ball. Whether you have a red stripe or not."

"But I'm a tour ball trapped inside a range ball's body," pleaded Bogey. "Don't you see? I need your help! Nobody believes me."

Dr. Ballpin had heard some doozy excuses before but nothing as hilarious as this one. That's why he offered to make Bogey's lips bigger instead. Bogey wasn't interested. He was too busy watching his ambition roll away. He was running out of time...

"Hey, Ma. Hey, Pa... I can't fall asleep!"
"Good night, Bogey!" said Ma and Pa Ballton.
Sleep?... Fuhget about it as Libber would say.
That night, Bogey...

and flipped...

He rotated...

...spun...

... and finally rolled off his bed and landed on his head!

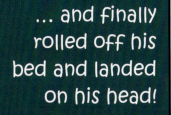

and flopped...

Bogey looked worse than a five day old deflated party balloon on the fringe. As if that wasn't bad enough, it was time to go to work...

Work was disastrous! Bogey tumbled off the tee four times before he was flubbed ten feet out into the range. The Bucket Bosses LOVED it. Bogey was too tired to care.

When he finally wobbled up to where his amigos were waiting, all Bogey could do was rub the side of his head - right on his sweet spot. He looked like a worn out range ball.

"This is more serious than I thought," said Libber. If it wasn't too late, he knew exactly who could fix Bogey. Tres agreed. It was totally worth the RISK!

They quickly pushed Bogey towards the fence, rolling him directly underneath the scariest sign EVER at the practice range.

BEWARE! No Range Balls Beyond This Point

"Wait... we can't do this!" cried Bogey as they rolled him through a hole in the fence. "I'll get caught without a disguise!"

"Don't worry," promised Tres. "We'll be back before anybody notices. And besides, it's totally worth the risk!..."

John The Ball Washer stood in front of the 2nd hole tee box.

"It's about time," said John, as they rolled Bogey up to him. "Nothing like a good cleansing. It will fix you right up!"

John reached down and picked up Bogey.

"Now it's up to you to take the first step," said John. "The Big Ball upstairs will do the rest!"

Bogey took a deep breath and stepped inside the ball plunger. John gave him three quick dunks before stopping. When he rolled out, his red stripe was brighter than ever!

"Wait a second!" said Bogey. "My stripe looks brand NEW!"

John explained to him how he needed to be Truthful about who he was. When he placed Bogey back down on the cart path, he handed him *The Rules of Golf* book. "Read this," said John. "You have to KNOW the rules... before you can PLAY the game!"

They quickly returned to the range without being noticed, wasting no time reading the book John gave Bogey. From cover to cover, the **Rules** inflated their lungs. The **Definitions** shocked their minds. The **Appendices** pumped up their hearts.

"ALL the answers have been in HERE this whole time!" Bogey realized. "What was I thinking?"

Just to make sure, they quickly measured Bogey with a paper measuring tape.

"One and three quarters of an inch," noted Tres in English.

With the help of Slim, the practice range flagstick, they weighed Bogey on a scale.

"One point six ounces," yelled Libber.

According to their math, Bogey met all the requirements in *The Rules of Golf* book.

"You DO realize what this means?!" asked Bogey. "The TRUTH will set us FREE!"

With one day left and no time to spare, Bogey bounced as fast as he could to Range Ball Headquarters, hopped up to the TOP FLOOR, and rolled straight into Mr. Ballbachev's office, the head range ball in charge.

He was sitting behind his ivory desk. The purple birth mark on his forehead matched the imprint of a 5-iron.

"There is nothing in this book that says I can't play!" declared Bogey as he held *The Rules of Golf* book high in the air.

Mr. Ballbachev responded with a thick accent. "I've already spoken to ze director at Top Flight School and have made all ze arrangements."

Mr. Ballbachev explained how the range knew this day would come. It had been written. They would allow Bogey to try out for the tour.

"But under one condition," said Mr. Ballbachev. "If you fails to make ze final cut, you'll find yourself on a one-way scooter to Pirate Island Golf where you'll spend ze rest of your long days as a Putt-Putt golf ball, <u>never</u> to be heard from again!"

Even though Bogey knew Mr. Ballbachev couldn't be trusted, it didn't take long for him to make his decision. "I'll do it!" he said.

"Congratulations, Mr. Ballton," said Mr. Ballbachev. "And good luck at Top Flight School. You certainly are going to need it!"

Overshooting the front door, Bogey CRASHED through the living room window and yelled, "MA - PA!" Of course, they were sitting right in front of him... now covered in broken glass.

He explained how he didn't need the can of spray paint after all. The way the rules were written, he could just... **Be Himself!**

"Everything's changed!" said Bogey. "Mr. Ballbachev even filled out the application for *Top Flight School*! He agreed to let me go!"

"Well, just promise me you'll always be Truthful and never forget where you came from," said Pa Ballton.

"I know, Pa!" agreed Bogey. "I'm honored to be a range ball now."

"I'm so proud of you, my little cotton ball," said Ma Ballton. "But before you get too big for your stripe... you need to straighten up that room of yours in the morning. And by the way, young man, you're going to pay for that window out of YOUR allowance!"

All Bogey could say was... "UhhggG!"

"Excuse me?" said Ma Ballton.

"Yes, ma'am..."

"Good night, Bogey."

(Till our next tee time!...)

...Rrff!

GLOSSARY OF GOLF TERMS

A

Address - The golfer's position when preparing to hit the ball. Not... "Hello, ball."

Albatross - A hole completed in three shots less than par. Very rare (like a hole-n-1).

B

Birdie - A hole competed in one-under par.

Bogey - A hole completed in one-over par.

Bunker - It's not "The Beach, Trap, Sand Trap". It's a hazard. An area in ground, usually a depression filled with sand.

C

Cart Path - Usually an asphalt, concrete, dirt or stone path that may connect the teeing ground to the green.

Chip - A short shot played around the green, usually with a short iron such as a 9-iron, pitching wedge or a sand wedge.

Cup - see "Hole".

D

Divot - A chunk of turf dug up when a club strikes the ground. Bogey's pet.

Draw - A shot with a slight, controlled curve through the air from right to left (for right-handed players).

F

Fade - A shot with a slight, controlled curve through the air from left to right (for right-handed players).

Fairway - The closely cut grass and easiest route between the tee and green.

Flagstick - is not a "Flagpole, Pin or Stick". It's a flagstick. A slender pole with a flag usually about 7 feet tall, marking the position of the hole on the green.

Flub - also "Dub, Duff, Dip, Chili, Top". When the bottom of a golf club strikes the top of a ball and causes the ball to immediately land on the ground.

Fore - The word shouted to warn golfers they are in danger of being hit by a ball.

Fried Egg - A ball in a bunker that is half buried in the sand and resembles a fried egg.

Fringe - also "Apron, Collar, Frog Hair". The short grass that separates the putting green from the rough or fairway.

G

Green - also "Putting Green". The closely cut area of grass where the flagstick and hole are located.

H

Hacker - also "Chopper, Duffer". Just a bad golfer.

Hole - also "Cup". A 4¼ inch diameter hole on the green into which the ball is played.

Hook - A shot that curves sharply from right to left in the air (for right-handed players).

L

Libber Tee - also "Liberty". Bogey's best friend. The quality or state of being free. The power to do as one pleases.

Lie - The position in which a ball comes to rest on the ground.

Lost Ball - A ball that cannot be found within 5 minutes of beginning the search.

LPGA - (Ladies Professional Golf Association) is the organization formed to organize and promote women in the game of golf. Founded in 1950.

P

Par - The number of shots an accomplished player is expected to make on a hole.

PGA - (Professional Golfers' Association) is the largest working sports organization in the world, comprised of more than 28,000 dedicated men and women promoting the game of golf to everyone, everywhere. Founded in 1916.

PGA TOUR - is an organization of professional golfers.

Practice Range - also "Driving Range, Range". Area where Bogey works, separate from the golf course, designated area for the practice of hitting golf balls.

Putt - A shot intended to make a ball roll, usually on the green.

R

Range Ball - also "Practice Ball". Golf ball used on the driving range, usually striped or marked to easily distinguish it from regular golf balls.

Rough - The longer grass bordering the fairway.

Rules - The world of golf is run by the *R & A Rules Limited* and the United States Golf Association *(USGA)*. Local rules may be decided by a club to address peculiarities on its course or for certain tournaments.

S

Scorecard - A card used to record scores during a round of golf.

Scratch - A player with a zero (0) handicap.

Slice - also "Banana Ball". A shot that curves sharply from left to right in the air (for right-handed players).

Sweet Spot - The solid spot on a ball or clubface that allows for a better shot.

T

Tee - also "Peg". A wooden or plastic device used to set the ball above the ground (maximum length is 4"); also, short for teeing ground. The area where the first shots at each hole are played.

Teeing Ground - Sometimes referred to as the Tee Box. A designated area where the first shot at each hole is played.

Trap - It's not the "The Beach or The Sand Trap". It's called a bunker and is a hazard. An area in ground, usually a depression filled with sand. See "Bunker".

Tres Wood - pronounced "trace", Spanish for three. Bogey's best friend. A club with a long shaft used for hitting long shots off the tee or fairway.

Truthful - The quality or property of keeping close to fact and avoiding distortion or misrepresentation.

Waggle - A movement or motion of the club for the purpose to stay calm and relaxed before hitting the ball.

The Tee Box

Discussion Topics for Parents & Instructors

Having a strong desire for advancement or success and to achieve a particular goal in life is the definition of ambition. As adults, we must teach and encourage our children the importance of having ambition and goals.

In this first volume, Bogey discovers one of the most important Bogeyisms in life. The act of being Truthful. Truthful means to tell or be disposed to telling the truth. Whether it is being Truthful about who you are and embracing your differences like Bogey did, or when playing a unique game such as Golf, where it requires players to impose the rules on themselves, we must always be Truthful. For example, when you record your score in golf, it is up to you and the other players to be Truthful. If you are not, it hurts all the people around you and your reputation. Being Truthful is fundamental to the game of golf and life.

Young people from all backgrounds need to recognize the importance of being Truthful on and off the golf course. Through rules and competition, hard work and practice, focus and discipline, and learning to win and lose, the lessons we learn by playing golf will forever impact our lives!

Discussion Questions:

- How is Bogey different from other balls? How are you different from other kids? What are your strengths?
- Why did Bogey want to cover up his red stripe?
- What lesson did Bogey learn?
- When do you need to be Truthful? Are there times others have not been Truthful with you? How did that make you feel?
- What Does Bogey want to do with his life? What do you want to do with your life?